Robert Saxton was born in Nottingham in 1952. He lives in north London, and is currently the editorial director of an illustrated book publishing company. He is the author of four previous books of poetry: from Enitharmon, *The Promise Clinic* (1994); and from Carcanet/Oxford*Poets*, *Manganese* (2003), *Local Honey* (2007) and *Hesiod's Calendar* (2010). He is also represented in Faber's *Poetry Introduction 7* and Carcanet's *Oxford Poets 2001* anthology. In 2001 he won the Keats-Shelley Memorial Association's poetry prize for 'The Nightingale Broadcasts'. See www.robertsaxton.co.uk for more information.

Robert Saxton

The China Shop Pictures

Shearsman Books

First published in the United Kingdom in 2012 by
Shearsman Books
50 Westons Hill Drive
Emersons Green
BRISTOL
BS16 7DF

Shearsman Books Ltd Registered Office
30–31 St. James Place, Mangotsfield, Bristol BS16 9JB
(this address not for correspondence)

www.shearsman.com

ISBN 978-1-84861-256-3

Acknowledgements

Thanks are due to the editors of the following publications and websites
where some of these poems first appeared:
Magazines: *PN Review, Poetry London, Poetry Review, Shearsman*
Websites: *Bow Wow Shop, Tower*

'Sea Walker' won a commendation in the
Troubadour Poetry Competition 2010.

'Ermenonville' is based on a passage in Gérard de Nerval's novella,
Sylvie (1853), acknowledged by Proust as an influence.

Contents

for my dear friend Peggy

and for my dear father, Colin

The Floating Village

Mayfly Menopause

However bad things are, they're far from worst.
Our pond's well pleased, beneath the star of best.
Our worsenings wave goodnight, quiet in the west.

Down in the flesh our mystery spins its time.
Our prizes shrink, disdainful in their game.
The beast inside us strokes us—courteous, tame.

The mountain clamps its average to a mound,
mismatch of muses, in a double grind.
We're dust but love the breezes of the mind.

No lion, drinking, stops to check its mane,
no soup aspires to settle in its spoon.
The love we longed for would have foxed our moon.

We're nice enough for both—truthful and kind.
We're dust but love the breezes of the mind.

On First Looking into a Second-hand Satchel

South Island

Sonnets, like egrets, have recently been
extending their range. We've spotted them of late
in flooded workings, in river sallows, on saltmarshes,
on heathlands. So beautiful—whitely defiant

beneath a pewter sky, proud of their angles,
forever patient, reserving their power of flight.
At times you'll even see them on cliff-tops
where the wind might have been a disincentive.

They're like suppositions before they're supposed—
ghosts, you might say, though indisputably *there*,
the super-efficient surrogates of souls.

Into our ken swims a new science of the sonnet ...
with terms like axillary, speculum, charm,
singularity, thorax and pendentive.

Narrow Straits

Where sonnets gather, manners have become
more formal. There's a tra, there's a tralee,
there's a fool, there's a king, there's a quiet grandee—
and all that's just for the opening ceremony.

Your teeth have dropped out before you're ready
for the first kiss. Sonneteers are always
offering each other precedence, so
no one actually ventures onto the stile,

and so the queue lengthens, frustratingly.
From the top step: an unimagined heaven,
suddenly lost as you drop to the other side.

That night you scribble away in your attic:
'Modern sonnets tend to have a jagged head
and a formidable tail, like a crocodile.'

North Island

They'll eat you alive with a satisfying snap
of the jaws, or fling you across the river.
There's a meal that brings wisdom, a bellyful
of acids corroding illusion, a protractor

in the throat of a jumbled pencil case.
We refuse to learn until it's many loves
too late—meanwhile we're fit and free,
one foot in school and one foot in the rave.

'For true appreciation think of the tail
as the head, and vice versa'—or a bulging
battered satchel stretching taut its long loop

on a lonely cliff-top walk amid the gulls'
cries in the wind, and a glimpse of a Dutchman
flying through a door without an architrave.

On Wicklow Fells

Argan Spraint, a shepherd's son, knew the constellations
before he knew the alphabet. One sheep, valiant against
predators, he named O'Ryan.

The fells of Wicklow teem with knitted sheep.
Our cottage mumbles in its cap of slate.
A stranger dances, gravely, on the grate.

The werewolf digs its den in human sleep.
A bear, with a grin, pours honey on the dawn,
your dewpond. A soot-speck fills your yawn.

The hills of Wicklow broil with ravelled sheep.
Some golf we played before our furze was burned.
Some gains we got before our lack was learned.

Fumbleton Farm

Good wife, I've stabled the plough.
Ribbons, like robins, deck the dray.
Mummers, roll over—stick the play!

Husband, your coat's besmirched by gulls.
Here's a clutch of golden rules
for the hayloft when my badge runs gules.

It's pigskin tight, the milkmaid's ring,
a peppermint on a farmer's tongue.
Drowned harvest proves the prayer book wrong.

You fling your stride beyond my ken.
Our hearth's out in the rain, forlorn—
a quail's nest in a crop of corn.

Down on the farm we all make do,
in the silence of prayer. *Too-whit too-whoo!*

The Circulating Library

Two equine-equestrian pictures, with appended verse commentaries

For the dark riders of the spiritual frontier

Every night a dozen or so wild horses, souls of the wisest books, silently move in towards the red-glowing ash-mound of the campfire, to drink from quiet minds. Clouds know what rain knew once but can no longer remember. Yet splashes they could never imagine, the raindrop's enlightenment, a brilliant haiku in an epic of tedium. When the storyteller pauses mid-flow for a punctuating silence, some endure suspense, while others, with relief, hear the tale, then its people, their pressures on our minds, and all the world and all its winds, gallop off, thunderously at first, then quietening into silence, swallowed into the living black centre of the wilderness where horses gather, neigh greetings to each other, discover they can think, and read, and speak, but need to find a better way to teach.

> *Cold starry night*   *blackboard of night*
> *horses below*   *chalk of snow*
> *their minds alight*   *the true the trite*
> *with all they know*   *and the cold rainbow.*

*

They linger still in our darkness, long after supper is over. We wonder how they can help us, because surely they can, and wish to, surely. They are like regrets, or in another mood the mistakes behind regrets, or the uncertainties behind mistakes. Our understanding is to our sickness as the weather is to our beloved valley—though many of us might imagine the opposite. So precarious are our myths, a stallion can take the place of a patriarch and be more intimate, on account of being a little less human. The Muybridge file lies unopened in some forgotten corner of the mind. Gusto is a wild cry, like 'Geronimo!' Acolytes occasionally take to the saddle, not in the sacred shows, but galloping hard between monasteries, carrying a thought before it has time to stiffen.

Wise is the animal   that only thin air
that needs no hands   sustains its ride—
and coming to a wall   vaulting despair
instantly understands   to the other side.

Sauve qui peut

Time's arrow has transfixed me to my desk.
Yellow brick makes the road more picturesque.

Your coat's a carpet, riding towards the door.
The sky's a blank: the ceiling loves the floor.

*

A gold purse, heart-shaped, the size of the palm
of your hand, hangs from your bag like a charm,

first as the usual hostage to ruthless greed,
then brandished as an amulet, selfless seed

of insouciance in the bustling market square.
Snatchers and snippers melt into thin air,

like love or time. Its value's what you choose:
you only keep what you could bear to lose.

*

Stairs are more dangerous, so tense all day,
with landings where we think, then turn away.

Bed beckons, softening what we share in sleep,
too small for all the life we'd love to keep.

The Lion Park

At the Savile Club, 1920s

Dry, flickering storms make this pavilion stronger.
Eminent members gravely appraise the danger.
A hornet in the lion park: literary stranger.

More comfortable on farms, or wetlands, fowling,
soldiering bravely under a cloud-borne ceiling,
terrestrial Orion in the front line of feeling.

His name? Hardy or Yeats—what does it matter?
Trained in the poppyfields of the *Bhagavad-Gita*,
he infiltrates breakfast armed with rhyme and metre.

Our gnat-bites drive such countrymen insane—
the metropolis yields by far the worst contusion.
Idly we entrust to a slap each squashed allusion

like a fly on a table inspiring some damp nocturnal,
the educated voice of a flood obsessed by a funnel,
a wartime meeting with a stranger in a shadowy tunnel.

There's a squirrel at the roots of national progress, gnawing.
Every Rolls-Royce Silver Cloud has a magic earring.
There's a rug-beating zephyr: celestial engineering.

She lost the thing in a fumble-fest one spring evening,
a sudden frost bringing love to the lilac, stiffening.
The adder lay quiet. The nightingale was deafening.

Discovered, he confessed to his once and future darling,
committed to pigeon post a flight of healing—
in the eye of the riot, oasis of single dealing.

At Wexford Cathedral, among ghosts of martyrs,
a stonecutter, chiselling a cave for himself in a buttress,
fathered a mooncalf on a flowerless mattress.

The long bumpy road dismantles the rickety wagon.
Make yourself big when you notice the distant dragon.

Four Feather Falls

An encounter with a feather-lined overcoat

The prime minister visits schools, and dinner ladies,
his overcoat too limp and lean to feed us:
we don't expect compassion from our leaders.

In the cloakroom, the ghost of a snowy owl,
a skeleton humoured at the draper's ball,
a coward's Christmas: white feathers for all.

A sweet girl, sat backwards on a prefect's chair,
reflecting on the Establishment's allure,
has been passed over for the prefecture.

What's the least number of feathers he would miss,
the eye being keenest in a rival house?
The tipping point's one tiny Arctic mouse.

It streaks behind the wainscot in a panic,
an elfin thumb at large in a giant's book.
Safety is more a rainbow than a nook.

A crock's a cairn of trouble on a map,
with devil winds, a compass in a cage of rope.
What do heroes do once they've slept with the dragon?

            Mope.

The foreign office from its park of spies
taps out the morning chorus to our wars.
Orders get through, in code, inscribed on spores.

At the big house where waitresses put on airs
a cocktail waitress is even luckier. Bores
needn't bother. Good swimmers need no oars.

Each fling's a fledgling, nobody's escutcheon,
a pierced heart lurking beneath the lichen
of a venerable oak: the woodpile in the kitchen.

Her only family is a loveless bad half-sister,
a cuckoo chick hardwired to evict her
from a nest she never knew. An eagle picked her:

a gladiator-artist flinging his net
to catch a generation, talentless and tight—
the pool so splashy all the summer night.

The China Shop Pictures

There's evidence of contact in the glues—
untoward incident, intemperate phrase.
The gift shop's magic shield's a crackle-glaze.

The whiplash tail's the thing you want to watch,
mad python's thwack a shelf-length from the flitch.
Some willowy dream will crash—the question's which?

Cuff 'im! Lasso the snout and staunch the riot,
rampage of drivelling culture in the gut.
It's a knocking-shop for an existential rut.

Muck in and grab the vandal's big brass ring.
Cosset the wounded king but cull the kong.
A headache's cool: a bellyache's all wrong.

If the geisha's haiku picnic goes ahead
as planned, in the meadow, unleash your healing word.
Insinuate the lamb in the thundering herd.

We're fools to think of cherry and pine as tame,
it's muscle that strings the gardener in his prime.
Wholeness is yesterday, the stench of time.

The moment's drunkenness is rocket fuel,
shrinking the manhood of the golden mile.
When will the herd parade in single file?

Only when Darwin learns to speak Chinese
and dragons emulate the geisha's poise,
hungry enough to swallow bestial noise.

Enamel's the coward's way, though it sells,
being safer in alleyways than porcelain bowls.
Smart sweethearts know you haven't paid in souls.

Awkwardly turning, caught in mid-air like a ball,
the lowliest bowl is now most mythical—
like the world-shaking, china-shattering bull.

The Crying of Lot 45

A collection of Jacobite wine glasses

Rain scarifies the sobering firth
yet here's a moth, emergent wraith,
alive, aloft—marvel of faith.

On a thistle next, in the threatening dawn
which leaches colours from its crown,
a goldfinch gently touches down.

'Fiat.' From loyal hearts such words
drop their cascade of native seeds
on fields choked with invasive weeds.

'Redeat.' Below the world's black rim
our sun flies on its voyage home,
with light for all and news of Rome.

And next, the rose, whose folded blade
is wrapped inside a soft white bud—
the diamond-point has drawn its blood.

This pair of compasses is one
we wield to toast the unfaltering line,
uptilting our communion's wine.

Next comes the odd one out, a cat
playing bagpipes: for a groat
the engraver has turned coat.

Oak leaves conceal a caterpillar,
feeding itself up for war,
munching the drapery of its lair.

Unclenched in the pilgrim's vale of hurt,
a sunflower rallies when clouds part,
buttonhole of the brimful heart.

And here's the rightful king, a man
refreshed with love, though wisdom-worn—
a face to follow, not to mourn.

Our prayer-hymn rises like the moon,
each breastplate girded in a glen
glistening with certainty: 'Amen.'

A star above the embattled tower
calls across the water: friends are here.

Some stems have an air-twist, some a tear.

Zanzibar Towers

The spice box loves its secret hinges,
like a horse's magic handles.
I fiddle with the thing in concerts,
leaving tear stains on my fingers.
No one contradicts my fables,
no one understands my wishes.

The spice box freshens mouldering wishes,
sneezing through the butler's binges,
scattering fresh-laid straw in stables
near the housemaid's thrice-used candles
where the scent of patchouli lingers,
masking lunchtime's chicken giblets.

The spice box has its drawer of giblets,
cool, as if on plain white dishes,
gratuities for carol singers
in the choir whose breathing conjures
anthems wound off creaky spindles,
marquetry of vestry tables.

The spice box, six times, turns its tables,
silver hair in golden lockets,
saints grown skywards from their sandals,
ice art exhibiting earlier fishes,
farmers rioting over henges,
waders filled from clouds by anglers.

The spice box, tracing cooks to anglers
dressing flies with glints and sables,
deals a dawn of ruthless lunges.

Nets shoot out on home-made rockets.
Gamekeepers, born to be suspicious
of boys with bumps and men with bundles,

drag their confiscated bundles
to the kitchen, where the anglers
and the cooks marvel at delicious-
looking salmon, beyond labels.
Silently luck blesses their banquets,
lures and loves, like well-oiled hinges—

mustards, gingers, congress of lockets,
candles coy on groaning tables,
fragrant fingers, red-raw dishes.

Highway of Diamonds

Pale Shadow (his operational name)
was an expert witness, often
taking the stand in cases where
Regina fought culture crime
of every monstrous stripe and hue—
plagiarism, forgery,
malfeasance, arrhythmia,
cliché. Regina was his muse.

A gangster/art film director
in bed with the Cornish mafia;
two collectors who discredited
each other's incunabula;
a punk Etonian drummer
spreading fear in the cabinet;
a harrier-shooting Rinpoche—
such were his juicy victories.

His expenses provided for
overnights in five-star hotels
but in fact he chose to flop down
in a room above The Green Man.
Studying his case notes in bed,
he might break off occasionally
to scribble some luminous thought
in a red school exercise book.

An actor who had based his Lear
on an aged queen of variety;
a biographer who had dreamed up
dozens of subsidiary lives;

a painter who copied himself
in secret, brushstroke by brushstroke;
the sly moth-breeder of Bayeux—
such were the ones that got away.

An Iranian girl, Sheba,
who was having an affair
with a concierge at The Swan,
passed him duplicate receipts
he submitted to the court bursary.
She loved them both, and jealousy,
his trademark theme, gnawed away
at all memories of his former self.

Melchior's

From the legendary star
down to the wandering shore:
the alien bought the store.

We rode here from afar.
Though timid folk withdraw
from the legendary star,

it's well within the law
so why the brouhaha?
The alien bought the store,

there's a heavenly door ajar,
a new trade corridor
from the legendary star.

Beetlejuice? Caveat emptor.
Try starfish caviar:
the alien bought the store.

Old man Melchior
doesn't find it so bizarre:
the alien bought the store
from the legendary star.

Strange Weather

Valdepeña, 25th April 1881

It happens at night, very rarely: a pup wind
schooling itself in mischief, the devil's air
scout in attendance, a backthrown bile-spit behind
him, apprentice meddler, fingers everywhere.

No marsh nor pond's immune. Though spawn and fry
seem gridlocked within their weed-bound world,
this wind convulses painfully to apply
its ascensionary lever. Skywards lives are hurled,

up into a primal, swirling gloop,
nursery of clouds, damp atticful of care.
Thermal cushions and nutritious soup-
rich miasmas keep these wee hearts beating there

till critical mass drops flesh from sky to plain
in a lordly benediction, as frog rain.

The Roof of the World

Imagine being a nun on a plateau
among lamas—if there's a lovelier life
I'd like to know. High above hills of tea
her cup's the sky, her brew's a solitary leaf

the porter brought and slipped into her prayers,
her dreams being locked. One door of the chapel
releases a prism of bright surprise.
A Himalayan morning greets her pearl:

red bull let loose among milk-swollen cows
that rub the sleep of ages from their eyes,
with hooves—a miracle that lifts the curse
from beasts not born to touch themselves with ease.

Sea Walker

Magpies of the West, drubbed by unparallel rains,
jerk eastwards with a rainbow-raiding wish.
You envy us our silks, our swords, our cranes,
our pillow books, our coastline and our fish.

Our laws give five the blame for any crime—
strict rule of hand whose fingers can't be fools.
Each fist of virtue staunches blood in time.
Murder's not done, except by elaborate rules.

You love our robes, pay dearly for the slub
of silk, its naked asymmetric bloom.
Each salad petal roofs a gourmet grub.
Now you're on stage we're in your dressing-room.

You roost on beaches, yearly on a whim.
Children fall soft and have no place to hide.
The point, for hours, is being about to swim,
or having *just* swum: octopus's bride.

We paddle in the shallows of devotion,
our gaze is still but hasn't learnt to stare.
We strive to love the surface of the ocean
more than its depths—it's much more debonair.

We're fishing for a dream that you'll agree to—
whoever sweats, or showers, or swims, or shaves.
Imagine a plastic bubble you can see through,
with a child inside. She's walking on the waves.

The Floating Village

Shore swindlers plot their pitch
on a far beach, landing their catch
of moonshine under an eye patch.

Those hills are a habitat of stars
too dim to give any cause
for panic's clash of oars.

Bare feet that never rocked
on yielding sand are circumspect:
timber's too personal to be wrecked.

Our evening's hymn is the nets
in the air, thrashing above cats
who swim—through shoals of gnats.

The possible thief's a spry,
strong breeze, just hearsay
at dawn, a sting of lake spray.

High on the lake's lap we sleep
on a raft of love, grief's isotope,
shy of all but the gentlest slope

and the flimsiest gate,
delicate within our moat,
no bell on the reed-thin goat.

Goats and Thistles

Passions of Earth and Sky

after Virgil, Georgics

Proem

(Book I, 1–12)

What makes the cornfield smile; under what cluster
of stars it's best to turn the soil or wed
the vine to the elm; how to keep cattle well-fed
in healthy flocks; and what bees need to muster

a sweet enough crop of honey from frugal flowers—
Maecenas, these are the themes I'll tackle soon.
O radiant lights of the firmament, Sun and Moon,
that lead the stars through heaven and rule men's hours.

O Ceres and Bacchus also, who by your grace
have exchanged the acorn for the plump wheat-ear
and blended new-found grape with sacred spring.

And you, Fauns, who in every country place
are so much loved—dance now, with Dryads, here
in my study. Of all your gifts I sing.

The Twilight of the Golden Age

(Book I, 118–146)

I.

For all the work of man and beast has achieved
in taming the land, still nature cannot refrain
from mischief—the Strymonian crane,
the incorrigible goose, the bitter-leaved,

fibrous chicory. Nor is the shade
of trees entirely harmless. Great Jove has willed
that a life of tillage or husbandry be filled
with trouble and toil. He it was who first made

art awaken the fields, relying on care
to sharpen men's wits. His subjects must not dream
in idleness. Before his reign no ploughman

subdued the soil, and no one would ever dare
to fence the plain—vile sacrilege! Earth's theme
was the common good: nature gave freely then.

II.

Jove it was who injected venom into snakes,
turned wolf packs into quarrelsome gangs of thieves,
swelled the ocean with storms, stripped honey from leaves,
hid fire from view and, for our virtue's sakes,

stopped up the wine that flowed in every stream—
so that experience, little by little, by taking
thought, might gain all kinds of skills, seeking
in shady furrow the peeping corn's pale gleam

and coaxing the diffident spark out of its flint
to grow a flame. And soon the rivers knew
the feel on their back of a hollow alder boat,

and mariners, conjuring stories from a hint
of stars, had grouped and named them for their crew,
making a night school of their time afloat.

III.

So swam into our ken the Pleiades,
the Hyades and Lycaon's daughter, the radiant Bear.
Soon men learned how to catch game with traps, snare
birds with lime, build workshops for honeybees.

To encircle wild beasts in coverts they trained
their hounds. It was not long too before one
man was casting for undulating trout upon
a leisurely stream, while another strained

to lift his dripping nets from stormy seas.
Then came unyielding iron, and the blade
of the rasping saw, a device contrived

to replace the wedge once hammered into trees
to split the wood. Art followed art. Toil made
the world we know, inspired by Want. Some thrived.

IV.

The goddess Ceres was the first to recruit
men to shuffle the earth with iron when
the acorns and arbutes of the sacred wood began
to fail, and Dodona withheld her fruit.

Soon, also, trouble fell upon the fields,
blighting lives—the baleful mildew feeding
on the corn and the lazy thistle seeding
itself everywhere, shrinking the harvest's yield.

And your hoe must be ever ready nowadays
to assail the weeds, your knife to chop down shade,
your prayers to invoke the rain, discourage floods,

your voice to scare the birds—or else you'll gaze
at the golden store of grain your neighbour's made,
so hungry you'll be shaking oak trees in the woods.

The Death of Caesar

(Book I, 424–514)

I.

By studying the impatient Sun and the volatile
moon you'll learn to outwit the weather's sleight
of hand—it will take more than a cloudless night
to fool you. When the new moon's crooked smile

returns, if within its pallid crescent
a dark mist hangs, discomfort lies in store
for farmers and mariners both: the rains will pour.
But if over her face, like a pubescent

girl's, there spreads a rosy blush, a stubborn wind
will blow. And if at her fourth rising she clips
across heaven sharp and bright, like a knife,

then all the following days until month's end
voyagers on placid waves can trust their ships,
each sailor in debt to the sea gods for his life.

II.

The Sun, also, rising from land or sea
each day, or sinking as blithe stars arise,
brings wisdom. When dawn shows cloudy skies,
a mist within his sharp periphery

warns us of showers—a south wind's sure to sweep
over icy ocean wastes to vent its spite
on trees, crops and herds. Or when spears of light
break out from morning clouds, or casting off sleep

the dawn goddess Aurora, delicate, pale,
forsakes the saffron couch of Tithonus,
inadequately will the vine leaves guard

the ripening grapes, for down will clatter hail,
like an arrow-storm, thick and merciless,
dancing on roofs, battering the vineyard.

III.

It's useful to watch the Sun retiring too,
for often we see fitful colours stain
his face. Dark green portends a threat of rain;
east winds will blow if you find a ruddy hue.

And if these accents merge with glowing fire,
nature will riot as leaden skies convulse
above tormented forests and fields, the pulse
of the world gone mad, the cloudscape haywire.

Let no one urge me to sail on a such a night,
or even row in the harbour. Yet if when the Sun
ignites or once more douses in dark the day

his solar disc glows pristine clear and bright,
there'll be no storm: our lapses are forgiven.
In a fine north wind the woods will gently sway.

IV.

In short, the Sun will give you helpful signs
of tomorrow: he never forecasts wrong.
Also, he warns of dark stirrings among
men—whispers of revolt, new battle-lines

drawn up, traitors competing in disgrace.
He (and no other) was moved to pity Rome
on the day great Caesar died. In gloom,
and then in darkness, he veiled his radiant face.

It seemed, to a godless age, the beginning
of endless night. But the Earth and the seas
produced bad omens also. Songbirds screeched,

and dogs ate dogs. Etna erupted, hurling
molten rocks on the fields of the Cyclopes.
White lava flowed, and city walls were breached.

V.

In Germany fierce battle-cries filled the air.
The Alps shook with earthquakes. Like deathly doves,
phantoms flitted at dusk. Through quiet groves
deafening voices boomed. Chaos raged everywhere.

Rivers stood still. The clouds rained spears.
Horror beyond words, animals uttered
human speech. Bronze statues, sweating, muttered
prayers. Sacred ivory figurines shed tears.

Whole forests were uprooted by the imperious Po,
whose frenzied current carried over the plain
cattle and stalls alike. Blood spouted from fountains.

And every hill-town rang with the echo
of howling wolves all night. Again and again,
comets flared; lightning twitched in the mountains.

VI.

And soon, at Philippi, a second time,
two Roman armies clashed while gods looked on,
allowing civil war as Macedon
and the Balkan plains were glutted with gore, a crime

against our people. One day in those fields
some farmer, ploughing, will turn up heroes' bones
and rusted javelins, amid phantom groans.
His hoe will strike empty helmets and broken shields.

O gods of our history, heroes unparalleled,
Romulus and Vesta, who guard Palatine
Rome and the Tuscan Tiber, do not destroy

our hope that a brave young prince will save a world
in ruins. Long enough has Aeneas' bloodline
paid in blood for Laomedon's perjury at Troy.

VII.

And long enough, surely, has the heavenly court
judged Caesar obsessed by earthly sovereignty.
Now right and wrong are inverted, as all can see.
War rules the world and sin's our favourite sport.

Our lands lie waste: the farmer's gone from sight.
Curved pruning tools are straightened to make swords.
Euphrates, Germany, fill with rampaging hordes.
Despite their treaties, neighbouring cities fight.

The war god runs amok, like a monster freed
from hell—just as, in a race, when the starting gates
are opened, out the thundering chariots stream

and lap by lap the horses gather speed
while the driver, panicked, powerless, concentrates
hard on the reins, yet cannot curb his team.

Animal Passions

(Book III, 209–283)

I.

The best way to keep a farm animal fit
is to curb its lust—it's the same battle
whether you're breeding horses or cattle.
For example, to train a bull, sequester it

in a lonely place miles from anywhere,
across a river, beyond a mountain ridge;
or make a large pen back home its hermitage.
The sight of the female's dangerous—beware

of the bull who echoes a lover's sigh,
his character turned wispy. Though virile,
he's weak of will—a ton of brainless brawn.

His memories of wood and pasture liquefy
and drain away. The cow with seductive guile
enjoys setting rivals clashing horn to horn.

II.

A lovely heifer grazes in the great wood
of Sila. Two gladiator bulls start
charging each other in turn, each desperate heart
pumping lust-fuelled hate, and spraying blood.

Black gore soon bathes their frames, and all the air
around fills with their mighty bellowing pain
as levelled horns pierce flesh again, again …
the forest echoing with the agony of the pair.

Then the vanquished one retires, as the sun sets,
to a private exile. He's full of shame
and hurt and loss—frustrated to have left

such humiliation unavenged. He frets,
glancing back at his stall, tearful and lame;
then quits his ancestral home, a beast bereft.

III.

But then with all his force of hate he keeps
himself awake all night in a knobbly den
among flints, restless, nibbling now and then
on prickly leaves and pointed sedges. Sleep's

unthinkable. At last with break of day
comes new resolve. He charges at a tree-
trunk as a test … then slowly, charily
he paws the sand, as prelude to the fray.

Advancing with colours raised, he rushes headlong
at his heedless foe—as when a wave of the sea,
starting to whiten, from the depths drawing power

and building up its curve, racing among
reefs, collapses like a mountain, deafeningly,
and hurls in the air a thick black shingle shower.

IV.

Every race on Earth, every man and beast,
all ocean tribes, all hoofed and feathered things,
burn with fires of passion. All feel Love's stings.
That's why the lioness leaves her cubs, to feast

her fleshly appetites as she prowls the plain.
The shapeless bear spreads havoc in the wood,
the boar deals death in his most amorous mood.
So does the tigress—any man's insane

who wanders alone in Libya. A rider knows
that shudder through the body of his horse
when a familiar scent wafts on the breeze.

No longer can mere rein or whip impose
his will. No beetling cliff can stem such force,
nor raging river—the torrent's crossed with ease.

V.

And no less driven is the tusky Sabine boar,
who paws the ground in front and rubs each side
hard on a tree-trunk to toughen his hide
against wounds—he'll bathe in *another*'s gore.

But what of our own kind, the love-struck youth?
Well, in the turmoil of the storm, at night,
he swims the straits. Above growls Heaven's might,
while the waves, dashing on cliffs, echo the truth

of mortality. His mother's helpless to call
him back to shore, and neither does the thought
of his lovely virgin sweetheart draped across

his untimely corpse, dying herself, forestall
his fate—though he'd be utterly distraught
if he'd a moment to prophesy such loss.

VI.

Now think of the spotted lynxes who drew
the chariot of Bacchus, vine-haired king,
from India. Think of the wolves, slobbering
with lust, and the wild dogs. Think of the hue

and cry of the stags, at other times so peaceful.
For madness, though, it's the mares who've taken
the prize. Venus inspired their frenzy when
the four Potnian mares, stallion-starved, excitable,

in a chariot race tore their master limb from limb—
Glaucus of Corinth, who wouldn't let them breed.
Irresistible is the mare resolved to mate,

against all odds—it's destiny, not whim.
Over Gargarus, in the clouds, they chase their steed,
and across the river Ascanius in full spate.

VII.

And once the flame has crept into their flesh
(mostly in spring), on a cliff-edge they gather
to face the Zephyrs, whole herds together,
drinking the breeze, so gentle and so fresh.

Miraculously made pregnant by the air,
dozens flee over plains and crags and dales
to the worst of our country's weather: gales,
saddening the sky with rain. Each ravished mare

then oozes from her groin the 'horse madness',
as shepherds call it. Down to the ground it drips,
slimy excretion of the wind's delights—

'hippomanes' in our language, a sticky mess
which wicked stepmothers with foam-flecked lips
collect to mix with herbs for secret rites.

Ermenonville

after Gérard de Nerval

25th August 1835:
the day after St Bartholomew's Day (the Festival of the Bow)

I.

I'd been travelling all night, arriving at the ball
as the lime trees were turning shades of blue
at their tops, remaining dark below. Now all
the guests were scattering, wan, like the retinue

of some defeated prince. Here and there the pale
spectre of a dress flitted across the dawn,
trailing wispy goodbyes. The village flute

was silent, like a remembered nightingale.
Girls talked about the dresses they had worn,
and released their hair. One tripped on a hornbeam root.

II.

Soon I found Sylvie, lively still, on the brink
of launching herself into a last quadrille
with a shy young man. She looked startled. Then at my wink
she beamed her familiar dark Athenian smile

and to her partner made polite apologies.
Arm in arm we strolled into the brightening day,
while awkwardly we traded each other's news

by the quietly burbling Thève. A sensuous breeze
from swathes and ricks brought whispers of new-mown hay—
nature may yield what a loved one's qualms refuse.

III.

'Sylvie, I've lost your love—I dare not doubt.'
'Dear friend,' she sighed. 'Things change, the moment flees.
Remember that book you so enthused about?
What was it called? *La Nouvelle Héloïse.*

"Every young girl who reads this book is lost."
Though that opening sentence scared me, I read on ...
Do you recall our dressing up in my aunt's

and uncle's wedding clothes? A dithering ghost,
you vanished. In Italy, Paris—our sweet dream gone—
there were prettier girls. No doubt there were amorous jaunts.'

IV.

'Sylvie, not even in Italy did I see
a single one whose eyes could match *your* eyes,
you dryad of the woods!' She replied: 'You flatter me ...
and from your failure to mention Paris I surmise

there's at least one special Parisian *mademoiselle.*'
Whereupon, in tears at her feet, I told her all
about my actress—from whom she could set me free.

She gave me a pitying look ... but then the spell
was broken by her brother, tipsy as usual.
'Till later,' she said, briskly offering her cheek to me.

V.

Having no need of sleep, I walked to Montagny
to see my uncle's house again. The green
shutters against the yellow façade filled me
with sadness—there was an air of quarantine

about the place. The farmer appeared with the key,
and flinging open the shutters I saw the past revive—
the walnut armoire skirted with a pointless frill,

engravings done after Boucher, delicately,
the wee dog stuffed I walked with when alive.
'As for the parrot,' I learned, 'she's chattering still.

VI.

'She lives with me—I adopted the saucy madam.'
We wandered into the garden where I recognised
the Eden I'd made for my toy-soldier Adam.
Then we entered the study and found my uncle's prized

library of books—his 'friends'—and the Roman relics
he'd dug up on the estate: medals, pottery.
I was keen to see the parrot—I'd loved her turn of phrase—

so we strolled to the farm. She was up to her old tricks,
imperiously calling for brandy. Her beady eye
set in wrinkled skin cast an old man's weary gaze.

VII.

With sadness I gave my thoughts to the life long gone
from these familiar scenes—the missing faces.
I needed to see Sylvie again, the only one
living who could bind me to these places.

It was noon, yet everyone was still in bed,
sleeping off the exertions of the ball. All was serene:
a perfect summer's day. I decided to kill

some time by walking along the road that led
through the oak-forest, whose shade was cool and green.
After two or three miles I would come to Ermenonville.

VIII.

The birds were silent—this was the midday lull.
The signposts were weathered, their lettering effaced,
yet I knew where I was as soon as the temple
appeared, between hazel trunks, widely spaced—

the Temple of Philosophy, left incomplete,
modelled on the shrine of the Tiburtine Sybil.
Beside a lake it stood, unworn by the flow

of time, being *built* worn—that was the conceit.
I'd paid fealty, on walks with my uncle,
to stone-carved names: Montaigne, Descartes, Rousseau …

IX.

All the great thinkers haunted this clump of pine,
shielded with rampant ivy all around.
The roses were throttled by raspberry and eglantine.
The bramble-battered steps were far from sound.

I'd seen honours awarded in this hallowed spot
to girls in white—the maidenly academy
whose virtues and knowledge claimed a fitting prize.

'As for the laurels, have they all been cut?'
the sweet girls sang. No, these shrubs from Italy
have simply perished, under our cloudy skies.

X.

Many such temples are crumbling towards their doom
as Nature besieges Art in its makeshift lairs.
Nearby, on the isle of poplars, stood Rousseau's tomb,
empty of its ashes—now with Voltaire's

in the Panthéon. O sage! You fed us the milk of the strong,
which we were all too weak to tolerate.
Those lessons you taught our fathers are forgotten,

like the meaning of the echoes of an ancient song.
Let's not despair: it might not be too late,
in our dying moments, to turn our eyes to the sun.

XI.

I glimpsed the castle, tranquil in its moat,
and the broad avenue which connected
the two halves of the village, with a dovecote
at each corner—the doves, I suspected,

had deserted their lodgings long ago. A greensward
stretched all around, with cedars, like a savannah.
There was the tower of the king's mistress Gabrielle

reflected in its artificial lake, starred
with dayflowers. Insects buzzed. A miasma
of sickness hung over the water, like a smell.

XII.

The air was treacherous, so I thought it best
to retreat to the Désert, and followed a trail
into that wilderness of sandstone and red dust
and on to the Heath, its green ferns dabbed with pale

pink broom. How desolate such places were!
Yet all these familiar scenes had once seemed
so full of charm, enlivened by Sylvie's

shouts of joy, her laughing *cris de cœur*,
the way she scampered like a goat, blasphemed,
and called me names, and the enchanting look in her eyes.

XIII.

She was still a wild, bare-footed creature then,
tanned despite the straw hat she liked to wear—
battered, but with a long scarlet ribbon
floating careless among those tresses of black hair.

We liked to drink milk together at a Swiss farm.
'What a pretty sweetheart you have, you lucky
Parisian!'—they all admired her so.

But no peasant would dare to offer her his arm,
for I was the only one she danced with, yearly,
on Bartholomew's Night, at the Festival of the Bow.

Autumn Leaves

The Doll's House

Dolls grow too big for their rooms and live outside,
or perhaps her home is a status-proud backdrop
scaled to appear a stroll away, or a gallop
on a wonderful pony she'd look so sweet bestride.

But when the house is open and fills your view,
that gate-click is your friend en route to a modelling
audition—or, if it's a Swiss house, yodelling.
Or she's housekeeping so fast to keep things new,

she's disappeared. She's dependably nice. In bed,
your cheek touched by her larger self's soft curls,
you cherish your collection of glimpses, like hen's

teeth, while adults, completing the half-said,
themselves at last, swing shut the doll's house walls—
though not before finding her tiny contact lens.

Well Past Bedtime

I've never understood how tired kids can get so naughty.
Is it that their energy, battling against fatigue,
ends up grotesquely misshapen? Ahead of the forty
heaven-sent winks, what you get is elves in forty-league

boots striding all over the furniture and snatching
the glasses off this year's so far most distinguished guest,
who sits on the sofa fielding a frozen smile, watching
the destruction. To bed now, boys!—we need our rest.

So peace at last descends, and it's like when the power fails
and you're bathed in candlelight and immune to the TV—
so refreshing!—and supper's a tin of beans, eaten cold.

The guest has smilingly risen from his bed of nails
and left. We miss them, a little. We push their door to see
them, asleep, amidst their bedroom's chaos—good as gold.

Reading and Memory

As I read, my Varifocals isolate
a porthole of sharpness cruising down the line,
shuttling far right and back its freight
of anyone's commuted into mine.

This is how intellectual property grows,
in relays of surprise like flowers of spring,
pristine as much as memory knows,
yet flaking paint in some forgotten wing.

And no one ever sees those specks of mind
in dust-clouds eddying round the broom
of sleep. As moorings, loosening, slip undone,

how frail a consolation when we find,
like hothouse roses in the wintry gloom,
some old book fresh again—the last but one.

Waterworks

All day I'm busy in the shop, but fretting
about the leak back there in the rusty tank.
There'll be a flood—the only question's when.
How will I cope? Not well. It's upsetting,

this sense of patient loss beyond my ken.
The water broods, the bedroom's dark and dank.
One tea-light smiles, remembering how to shine.
My vigil's long for a life overlapping mine.

Some locals seem undeterred by driving rain,
perhaps are even friendlier when it's wet.
I'm anxious to ignore the drip's refrain—
from chronic to acute downgrade the threat.

How high's the breach? How quick's the rising tide?
He's drowning. Let the customers decide.

Wanderer's Moon

A whisper in the birches tugs, *Why not?*
The night's our mystery, trembling on the brink
of logic, folding shame into its plot.
The rational moon between each wind-blown blink

withholds its censure even for as long
as it keeps its purpose, riding the high road
of adventure. You're weak in some ways, strong
in others. Here's the gift of a larger cloud.

Could the moon be the mirror or even the origin
of conscience? Stripped of the medal of day,
the heart's mad soldier churns adrenaline.
You're pulled along a soft yet trackless way,

free of the forward shadow of a life,
engloved in darkness—no glint on the knife.

Dawn Chorus

How consoling in the dark hours of sorrow,
this lyrical affirmation of the dawn.
And should their notes fall flat, for sure tomorrow
they'll be undeterred, the first daylit yawn

of the sleepless soul again invited
to gulp down breakfast juice of joyful song,
nourishing day by day the benighted
one with a natural remedy. Wrong!

A ruthless need primes many a dreamy wish.
Our genes rush to the mate veiled by the bride.
Beauty's competitive and won't be blamed.

These birds use the dawn chorus to establish
each morning whether any of them has died
in the night, leaving a territory unclaimed.

Winter Triptych

Barn Owl

Silence, in wings, comes at a cost:
in heavy rain you just can't fly.

Stalkers disband, give up the ghost.
Failing, no one can fathom why.

The dream they share, like a spring frost,
has melted back to fantasy.

In flight's the mode they love the most,
easeful, capsizing suddenly;

next, watchful on a nearby post,
even in the rain, in misery.

Kingfisher

When inland waters freeze, the coast
is your only hope. Worse than shy,

the fish are clamped in a cruel frost
or trapped in a paralysing pie

with a crust of ice. You'd be lost
at home—if you stayed, you'd die.

Yet callers come, and check your post,
your favourite branch, naïvely.

There's only a wink of pond at most
for your sprint of blue in their eye.

Waxwing

When berries fail, cold wastes are crossed
by armies, routed, braving the North Sea.

Home guard patrols catch the proud crests,
the cocoa-brown of a *congeries*,

perhaps even the red embossed
seals on the wings if they're lucky.

Shoppers dawdle. Brazen, engrossed,
in the busy carpark's rowan tree,

we feast. Yet fairy lights and frost
are all two latecomers will see.

Scarecrows

From desperation comes the fetish
        of unnecessary work: a second wash,
another dangled cork.

Lost things summon an urgent need
        even for redundant buttons or plaid—
soon they're all too abundant.

The truth of us is what we lack,
        since having stuff is our worst luck—
ill-chosen and more than enough.

Die Schöne Müllerin

The serious heraldry of the time that's come to stay

I've heard her
   on a hundred tongues
      flying a hundred songs.

I've grounded her
   so she's mine alone,
      sly nymph of the millstone.

The millstream trout
   scroll courtship songs
      on rippling tongues.

My daughter's
   heart is hard as stone—
      and so I mourn alone.

Autumn Leaves

Leaves, gold, yellow and brown,
sit on swirls of gravel—floating worries,
dead butterflies nobody misses,
the adjective shower behind the frown,
strewn wrappings of ancestral stories,
widowy husks of chrysalises.

And now I think back to my one lost
love, enduring, immovable stone
island weathered by wind and rain,
and as I weaken and reckon the cost,
I embrace the consolation: no one
will ever have her that young again.

After a minute or two I fetch the rake
with the long bamboo handle, settle
the thing in my hands, and swinging out to graze
the gravel lightly, for the gravel's sake
catch a few leaves in its tines and haul
them in, like a netful of dried-up days.

Island of Voices

A.m., p.m.

Good morning! The dare's well breakfasted on trust.
Your fingers wave goodbye to last night's fist,
unclenching to scribble your number, chance a tryst.

We meet as innocents, the slate wiped clean
before school starts, track record ours alone,
with miles of thanks for every classless clone.

Clean air, as racing drivers say, is what we taste,
fresh every morning, history's sins confessed,
revision done and dusted as we flunk the test

of the turning day, floundering between all or none
among social nuances, setting of a precious stone
whose workshop's dubious and whose worth's unknown.

Would cake adore a fork or die for a spoon?
Welcome to teatime, klutz. Good afternoon.

Teatime at the Athenaeum

We adults like to demonstrate just how cool
we are by walking in disguise among
kids, downloading hit singles, dissing school
and (my main point) hijacking the *speech* of the young—

phrases like 'That so isn't going to happen.'
And because kids nowadays mature so much quicker,
we're regressing. Rebels with Baby Gap on
squeal, 'Homework's pants,' and soon some trendy vicar

's spouting 'Nimbyism's pants' from his pulpit.
Boardrooms, and not only in advertising,
are coldshouldering *gravitas,* re-enacting the saga

of hothead Olympians defenestrating the time culprit
Cronus. Old age is pants. So it's hardly surprising
some of us cling to our power with the war-cry, 'Ga ga.'

Ornaments

There's an ornament in your room you've never seen—
perhaps a stallion with eels for a mane
or a grinning, lotus-squatting genie. Insane!

—to have such an object in your home, I mean.
It exudes all through the shortening afternoon
the sweat of Beelzebub's honeymoon.

Its adversary is your parian Bodhisattva
whose valleys, like a gopi's, fill with dew
in the heavenly dawn's all-merciful review.

Here, catch! Savour the warm talismanic glow,
its fragrance of virtue, like a desert shower.
Across the room (quick, look!) red eyeballs glower.

Fumbled? Broken? Glued? Love keeps things whole.
Pulverised, a genie will hunger for your soul.

Jedward

Destiny, of course, might love one less,
but which? Take that shield with the double boss
and feel its bumps. Intuit. Divine Rome's loss.

They're stumbling in the labyrinthine mess
some cruel god left. Aren't spells effective twice?
A name's revealed in the scurrying of mice.

Body and Soul

A redaction of W.H. Auden, 'No, Plato, No' (1973)

I can't imagine anything
on Earth I'd less like to be
than a disincarnate spirit—
with nothing to do but sing
the song of the stars eternally,
with only the Lord to hear it.

How tragic not to do human stuff
like chew or sip, or salivate
over a girl in a magazine
at the dentist's. It's tough
not being able to guess the weight
of a cake and win a soup-tureen

or gramophone at the summer
fête, or gleefully waddle around
in the park with a tireless dog
or great-nephew. What a bummer!
Little things too make my heart bound
with joy, my senses all agog:

smells of mint and musk and dung,
my grandpa's grave alive with moss,
the silence of a mended tap,
the hopeful muddles of the young,
that marvellous feeling when you toss
small change into a busker's cap.

God placed me exactly *here*—
give me one more decade please!
This sub-lunar world is a riot—
the clubs, the farms, the biosphere.
We drink, we snooze, play bridge, keep bees;
we write to keep our demons quiet.

Meanwhile, my organs slave away
without complaint, twenty-four/seven,
doing my will as the Lord designed.
It's a miracle—for I have to say,
I haven't a clue how in Heaven
they work. Can they read my mind?

Might they dream of another dimension,
released from the great 'I Am'?
Will they dance when my loved ones scatter
my ashes and cancel my pension?
Will they smile when Hamlet's just ham
and they're irresponsible matter?

Umbrella Dance

I'm here in the store to kick up a stink,
my dander's sky-high, I have to confess,
    I can't sleep a wink,
      or hear myself think.
This umbrella I've bought is a God-awful mess.

The handle has grooves, I tell you no lie,
where your fingers fit snug—but the hassle
    is that holding it high
      brings the Velcro tie
round in front of your face like a tassel.

I've tried twisting the stem to swing the thing round
but I think if I forced it I'd break it.
    So I'm here in the shop
      and I'm blowing my top,
if I still had my brolly I'd shake it.

Ah, you've swivelled the grip, there's a secret release,
you've adjusted the tie to the rear.
    You've brought back my peace—
      you look just like my niece!
You're a poppet, a genius, a dear!

Yes, umbrellas are prone to these modernist trends,
and it's hard if you live in the Stone Age.
    But I must make amends,
      oh, do let's be friends—
there's a heart that means well in this bone cage.

An umbrella's bones are fragile and scared,
for the wind can hurt more than the rain.
But when fangs have been bared
and your problems are shared,
you're ready for sunshine again.

The Real Thing

'You don't send men where you haven't sent the monkey.'
Moon landing conspiracy theorist

I sleep all alone,
I'm afraid of the phone,
I'm cold in my cushioned cocoon.
    Yet I do have a dear one
    (though hardly a near one)—
the monkey they left on the moon.

Enthroned in his crater,
he feeds me raw data,
like jam on a runcible spoon.
    He's handsome and brave,
    and I've made him my slave—
the monkey they left on the moon.

I'm lithe as a trout
(that's the yoga, no doubt),
though my mouth falls in pleats like a prune.
    And I'm pliably thumbed,
    which is why he succumbed—
the monkey they left on the moon.

No true heart is miffed
by a Valentine's gift,
and a lunar one's quite opportune.
    Sure, he'll save me some crust
    as a pledge of his trust—
the monkey they left on the moon.

From a drifting cloud's brink
the bright orb seems to wink
like a space pirate's stolen doubloon,
    and it bribes me to yearn
    that he'll safely return,
and tomorrow would not be too soon,

and it tips me its gleam
like a prospector's dream,
before banking to Earth in a swoon,
    and it funds me to hope
    he'll be learning to cope—
the monkey they left on the moon.

Shutter Buddy Boogie

I'm a shutter buddy, and I always have been.
    I pride myself on my skills,
    both social and technical.
I've been shuttering since I was seventeen.
    I can do plain, I can do fancy frills.

I'm a shutter buddy, and I'm Captain Keen.
    The strong win merit, redeeming the demure.
    Anybody pregnant knows I'm on call—
I'll sweat for them, an affable machine
    to close the shutter, keeping their bairn secure.

I'm a shutter buddy, and I'll always wait
    for any lovely, ladylike mum-to-be
    whose in-tray's impossibly tall.
Keyholder, yes, but you can't pull down the gate.
    Don't worry, help's on hand, you're safe with me.

I'm a shutter buddy, and loth to accept a nightcap.
    A thankyou's brushed off with a graceful mumble.
    Inwardly I'm having a ball.
Sinewy and caring, I pump iron in the gap,
    slamming the grill with a flourish, rarely a stumble.

I'm a shutter buddy, with a midwife's understanding.
    Home birth, epidurals, baby names and scans—
    we're waxing lyrical
while the lift cranks up, chatting on the landing.
    Outside I sign the bumps of pregnant fans.

I'm a shutter buddy, and my ballpoint's Zorro,
    a rapier dancing in the Hollywood hills.
    My autograph's quite valuable.
Same time, same place, same shutter groupies, tomorrow.
    I can do plain, I can do fancy frills.

Ariel's Cloak
or
Why I'm Not Enamoured of *The Tempest*

Delusion bold! and how can it be wrought?
The garb he wears is black as death, the word
'*Invisible*' flames forth upon his chest.
> William Wordsworth, *The Prelude* (1850), vii 285–287

The Time Lord of the tackle and the gauze,
   faux magus, sanctioned in his theft of time,
unkennels his bearded voice for our applause.
   The monster's pleased with his adjusted slime,
the maiden with her hair. No curtain, of course—
   a thunder-flash launches the pantomime.
      Fiercely the thought police patrol their beat.
      Decorum keeps me spell-bound in my seat.

Yarely's the word I savour, meaning 'Quick!   Act I, Scene i
   Yank ropes, talk bilge and rush about the deck!'
'Yarely!' I yearn to yell, yob groundling's trick,
   when the conjurer stoops to extricate the speck   Act I, Scene ii
from his daughter's eye, so megalo-prolific.
   Sweet innocent, she frets about his wreck—
      those souls in danger, plump for a mercy mission.
      She wilts (me too) in the warp of his exposition.

It's time (why now?) to unspool the spangled spiel:
   who she and her father are, and how they came
to live this desert island dream for real
   (ha ha!), in a hundred-and-sixty lines of shame—
an endless, artless, tedious fictive squeal
   that cooks choice brains to mush on a heathen flame.
      The very minute that bids her ope her ear
      brings zeds to us both on a tide of loghorrea.

Can I remember a life before this play?
    Only dimly, through my apnoea, fathoms off,
like a drowned book. Vaudeville *boulevardier*,
    for God's sake abjure your magic now—it's rough
and unrehearsed. Do what a real castaway
        would do: steal their boat and hope it's idiot-proof.
            Enter the sprite. His feats don't make me feel good
            any more than the ersatz ham of that would-be Gielgud.

There's action but it hovers like a ghost
    in intensive care, too desperate to fly.
Nobody's in disguise, or spread on toast.
    Nobody's witty, nobody learns to cry.
No inland empire claims a spurious coast.
    Beauty's not dangerous: merely sugary-shy.
        When the sprite's informed of what he already knows,
        how should we feel? Cognisant, I suppose.

We're introduced to a savage, slobbering croton
    (remember, this is early *Dr Who*)
that even minced you wouldn't feed your goat on.
    The post-colonial thesis may be true,
a peg to hang a doctor's threadbare coat on,
    on the back of the door of a flooded Portaloo,
        but is it really theatre? Don't ask me.
        It clamps the mind and throws away the key.

'The wild wave, whist; foot it featly here, and there.'
    With a song for the prince amazed he's on dry land,
the sprite conjoins his wings, like hands in prayer.
    The prince, bereaved, struggles to understand

a ditty three parts mud and one part air.
    His father's coral and pearl? On a bed of sand?
        Ding-dong: the sea-nymphs hourly ring his knell.
        The famous sea-change weaves its winsome spell.

The sprite's invisible—an air-change hard to swallow.
    I see him—are my neighbours just as coarse?
This magic flute to me is stiff and hollow.
    Agnostic, I prod the illusion with too much force,
and it fails me: in a swamp of fact I wallow,
    too smart to believe two hunched men are a horse.
        To factual folk who are fazed by fume and fable
        his cloak's a lying, self-defeating label.

Then the prince and the conjurer's daughter fall in love—
    exchange of eyes, with wonder on both sides.
The sprite has given them a romantic shove,
    the conjurer to his inner crowd confides,
smug to hear the cooing of a conjured dove—
    or creaking rather. About the stage he strides,
        a tinsel tyrant. Inexorable it's not:
        he bans their match to inflate a flaccid plot.

Elsewhere a shipwrecked bunch of stuffed doublets—   Act II, Scene i
    a king, his brother, a duke, plus hangers-on—
are grazing on words. Two whisperers place bets
    on who'll speak first and stupidest, such cruel fun
flagging them as villains who'd have no regrets
    about worse harm than a puerile bitchathon.
        Now for a plot twist, dredged from the bardic deep:
        the sprite puts all but this dubious pair to sleep.

Then the duke, a blackguard and a self-confessed
        usurper, urges the king's brother to slay
the slumbering king by parking a sword in his chest.
        Lightly the crown would float the brother's way—
seduction of conscience by a destiny undressed.
        I catch an echo of the Scottish play,
                in a lighter vein, without any actual crime:
                the conjurer's sprite wakes the victim just in time.

Or rather he wakes his counsellor—concentrate!—
        who's dreaming of an island paradise
to outshine the Golden Age, a utopian state
        sans property, employment, weapons or dice—
pure nature, unblemished by lord or magistrate.
        The sprite wakes *him*, who wakes the king in a trice,
                who opening his eyes sees a brace of swords held high.
                They adlib: 'We heard weird noises.' So did I.

A butler, next, in a panic in a tropical storm,   Act II, Scene ii
        meets a sea-monster with four legs in a twist.
Two belong to a jester, minded to stay warm
        and dry beneath the croton. They all get pissed
once disentangled. The absurd tableau they form
        is worthy of an Irish existentialist.
                The butler has salted away a butt of sack,
                so the monster adores him—typical poet's *craic*!

In a sunnier scene the prince is carrying a log.   Act III, Scene i
        Even princes, for love, are happy to re-train.
Labourers win hearts. Wooing's an uphill slog.
        Yet this girl's more than willing to share the strain.

'I am your wife,' she gives him this wee jog,
   'if you will marry me.' How unusually sane!
      Never was bliss so wonderfully axiomatic.
      Her father frowns—the scene's a yawn: so static.

Then, behold, a nest of dung beetles near by—   Act III, Scene ii
   a shocking contrast. The three cupwits boast
of their bravery in drinking the island dry.
      Each empty moment's filled with an idiot toast
to random bile-soaked nonsense. Why, oh why?
      The Puritan in me gags—offended host.
         They'll cut the wizard's wezard with a knife,
         crown the butler king, 'ennoble' the girl. Pond life!

The sprite in a flying contraption picks his time
   to chip in, 'Thou liest!', so the fool cops the blame.
'He's above you!' I'm longing to shout (it's pantomime),
      but the stares would turn me to salt—this is no game,
it's a feast for the soul, and heckling's a cultural crime.
      A rowdy yell might dowse the eternal flame.
         Besides, if they raised their eyes, they'd refuse to see.
         He's audible, though—they follow his fiddle-de-dee.

The doublets are searching for the missing prince,   Act III, Scene iii
   with shrinking hopes—he surely must be drowned.
The plotters drop their regicidal hints—
   tonight will see the royal brother crowned.
Then a banquet materialises—guinea fowl, parsnips, quince—
   but fades before a single morsel's downed.
         The conjurer's sprite, as a harpy, winged, is visible.
         Now it's the conjurer no one sees. That's risible!

The sprite declaims, like a hanging judge, baritone
        and tremulous—or like a Dalek warlord,
invincible inside his cardboard cone.
        The Fates, he explains, are still at the drawing board,
devising trials for the villains for what they've done
        to the conjurer and his daughter—now restored
                to justice by the conjurer's own skills.
                Having landed his minnows, he has them by the gills.

The lovers, it seems, were promised a magic show,   Act IV, Scene i
        a 'trifle' of the conjurer's art they well deserve
for crowning their spiritual yes with a physical no.
        The nuptial feast is missing its hors d'oeuvre.
A fleshly snack would bring them serious woe—
        discord, blighted offspring. Hence their reserve.
                The conjurer can safely leave them out of sight,
                chaperoned by their fear of spousal blight.

The play within a play begins, the sprite
        having summoned a trio of divas out of nowhere.
Time stops. Hope shrinks. Intelligence takes flight.
        Exit sanity, pursued by a puff of air.
I called them divas only to be polite—
        actually they're spirits. I clutch the arms of my chair
                and brace myself for the surge of blinding pain,
                a million volts of nonsense through my brain.

Iris speaks first, the spirit with the saffron wings—
        of wheat and rye, of vetches, oats and pease.
She calls for the goddess Ceres, and down she swings,
        to a lawn, on a flower-bedecked trapeze.

They pamper the lovers with the opium of kings
      and queens—namely, a masque: a gruesome frieze
         of cold abstractions in a starched parade.
            In lieu of veins these divas have red braid.

There's a cameo from the 'highest queen of state',
      with very few lines and very little merit.
'Great Juno comes, I know her by her gait,'
      Ceres confides. Ever the literary ferret,
I feel my nose twitch: doggerel! Who would rate
      such couplets higher? No self-respecting poet.
         Some of the rhymes are hopelessly inexact.
         I pray to Jupiter: Help! Wrap up this act!

The prince, however, is thrilled. To conclude
      the show, Iris is sent to pair a charm
of naiads with some yokel reapers, rude
      mechanicals who've learned movement on a farm.
Ill-matched with the graceful nymphs, with crumbs of food
      in their beards, they jig the jig in wild alarm,
         then vanish: the conjurer's had a gloomy thought—
         his bursting ego swamps his little court.

He's remembered the drunken boobies and their scheme
      to take his life—he'll tie up this loose end.
The revels are over. Life's a wisp of steam.
      Could this be the beginning of the end?
My devoutly wished escape? The arrogant gleam
      in his eye is dull now. Odd for him to send
         the lovers to relax *inside his cell*!
         He's lost the plot. He's looking quite unwell.

The sprite last saw the drunken dimwits sprawling
        in a filthy pond. Like three dysfunctional frogs,
they blunder about onstage, then, falling
        over each other, come across fancy togs
draped by the sprite on a tree. That starts them brawling
        over who gets what. They try on a gown. Then dogs
                are set upon them—fairies in disguise.
                Wet drunks in drag! Bring on the custard pies.

The conjurer's himself again, supreme, advised   Act V, scene i
        by his elfin scout his project's going well.
The king and his followers are paralysed
        inside a magic circle near his cell.
Teleported by the sprite, they get chastised
        by the conjurer, who's loosening his spell
                so they can listen and think but still can't budge.
                'Disappearing' this dude has given him a crazy grudge.

A revolving stage cranks out its groaning grind—
        cleverer than just a curtain, I confess.
The conjurer knows exactly what we'll find:
        the sublimated lovers playing chess,
delighting in the thrill of mind on mind.
        The prince plays fair (obligation of *noblesse*),
                so gentle on this weird cerebral date:
                the one thing neither dares to do is mate.

The king is all remorse. The girl's agog
        at this brave new world—fine people like himself
(her learning curve would make a telling blog).
        A prince has plucked her from the ocean shelf,

and all is well—though still they cannot snog.
    The irritating conjurer and his elf
        are healers. Wedding in Naples, then to Milan:
        such is the conjurer's retirement plan.

He deals with the sailors (remember 'yarely'?—
    in magic bunks they've been sleeping all this time),
then with the croton. Is the beast forgiven? Barely.
    He releases the sprite—not to would be a crime.
The play is done for which we've all paid dearly—
    the conjurer owes us, though the debt's sub-prime.
        Sail fair, yon ship, on a sea like an inland lake—
        a tempest would be more than we could take.

The stage goes dark—thank Jove, the promised hour!   *Epilogue*
    The conjurer's all alone in a pool of light.
I feel a blessing coming on, a shower
    of rain in the waste land. Happiness writes white.
I'm like a virgin in a madman's tower—
    first tug on the ladder of locks is sheer delight.
        The night air! Friends! The pub! But first, the loo!
        To free him I must clap, I'm told. I do.

CPSIA information can be obtained at www.ICGtesting.com
Printed in the USA
LVOW132306181212

312282LV00002B/10/P